# DELITEFUL COLORING

# BLACK WOMEN ARE DOPE

## by Sandra Mcdyess

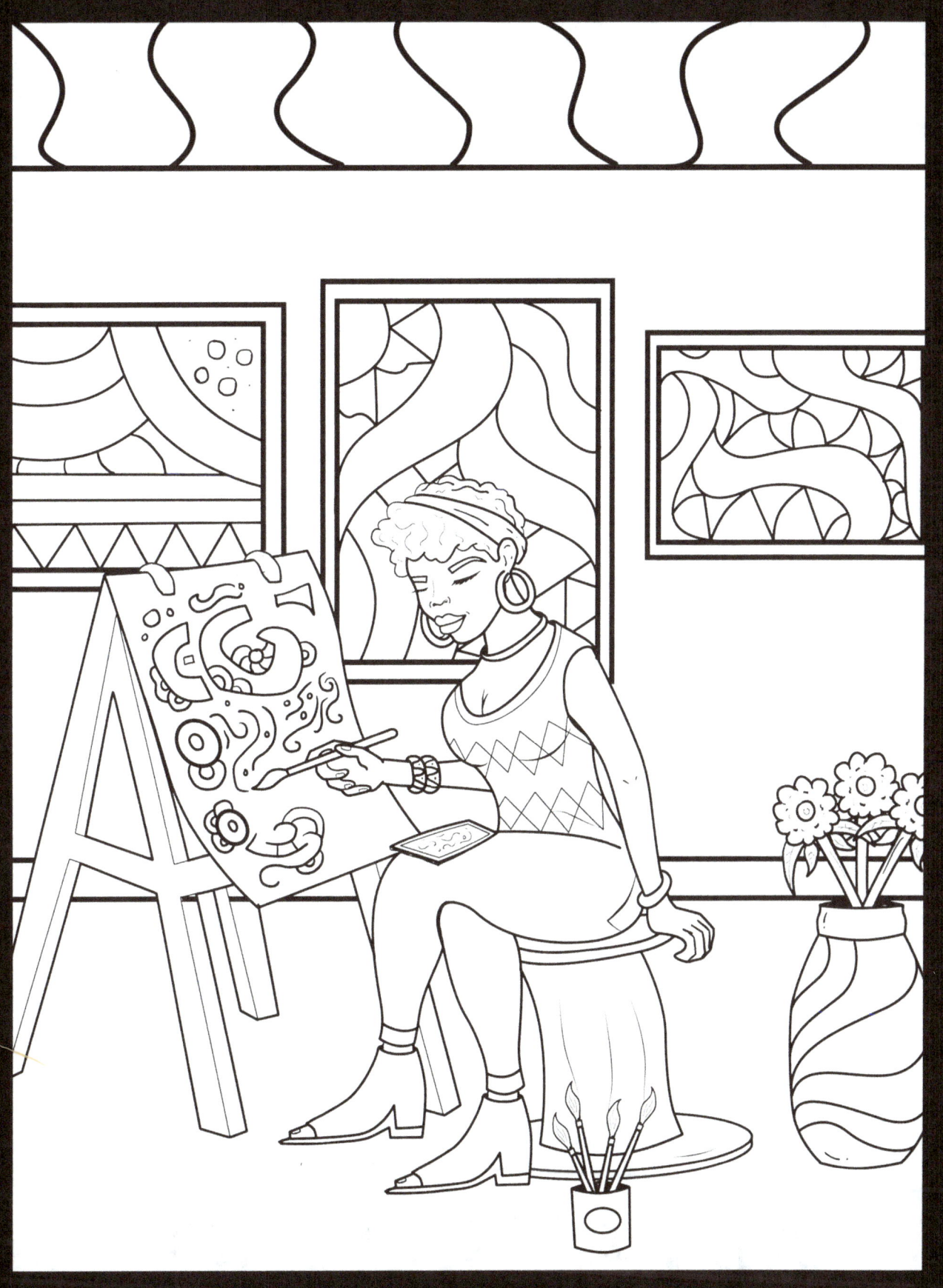

ARTIST STUDIO

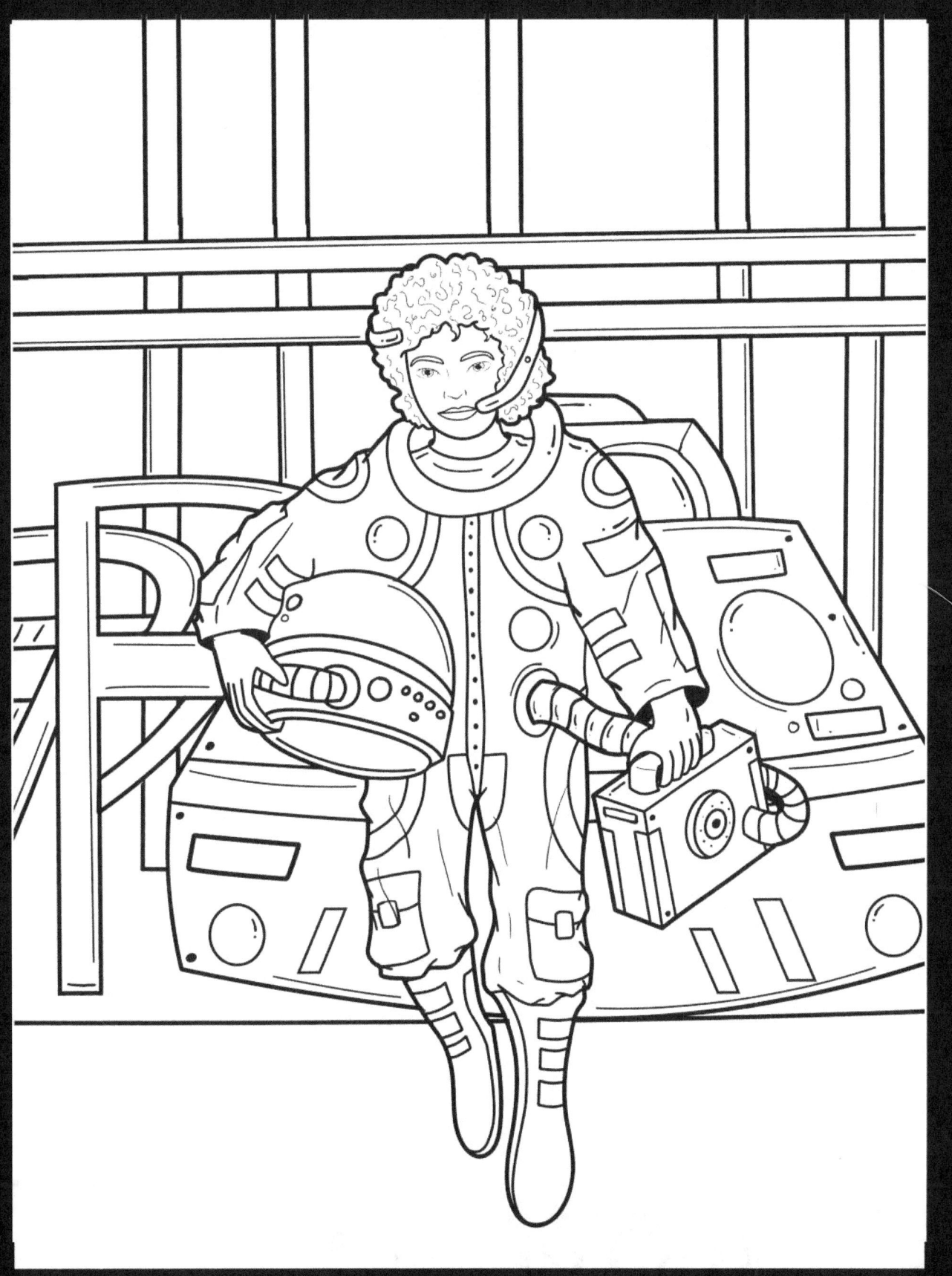

# ASTRONAUT

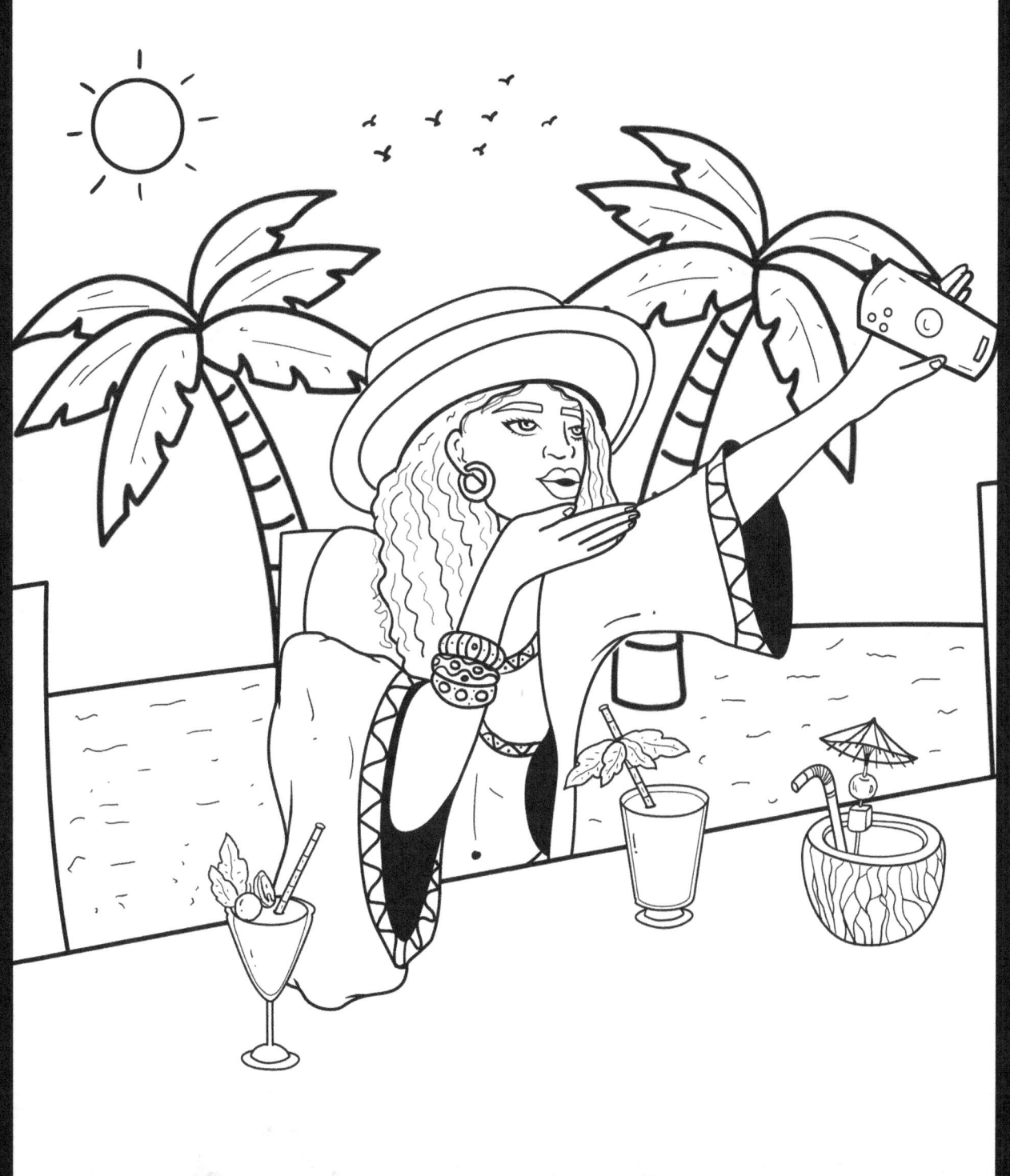

# AT THE BEACH

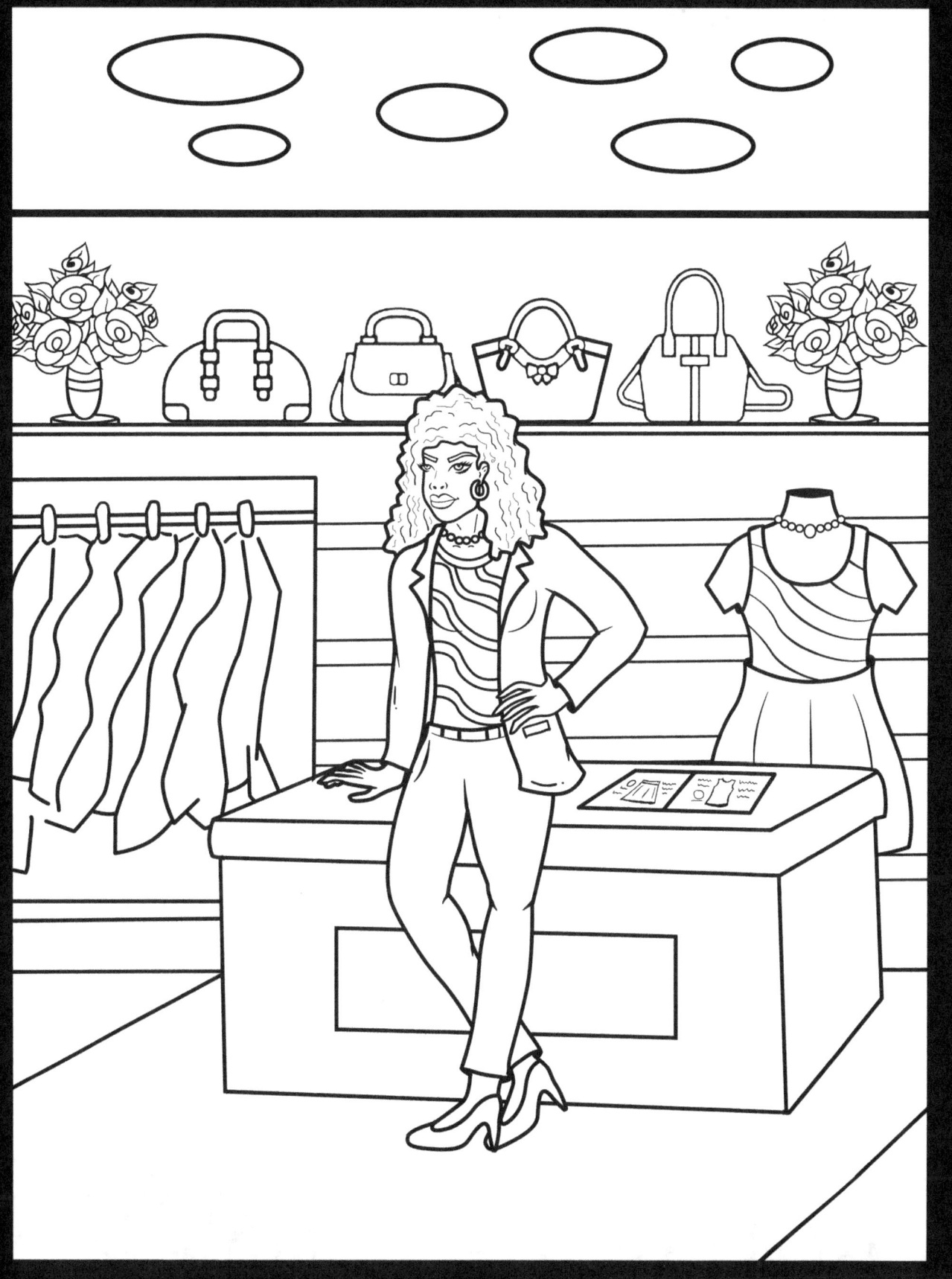

# BOUTIQUE OWNER

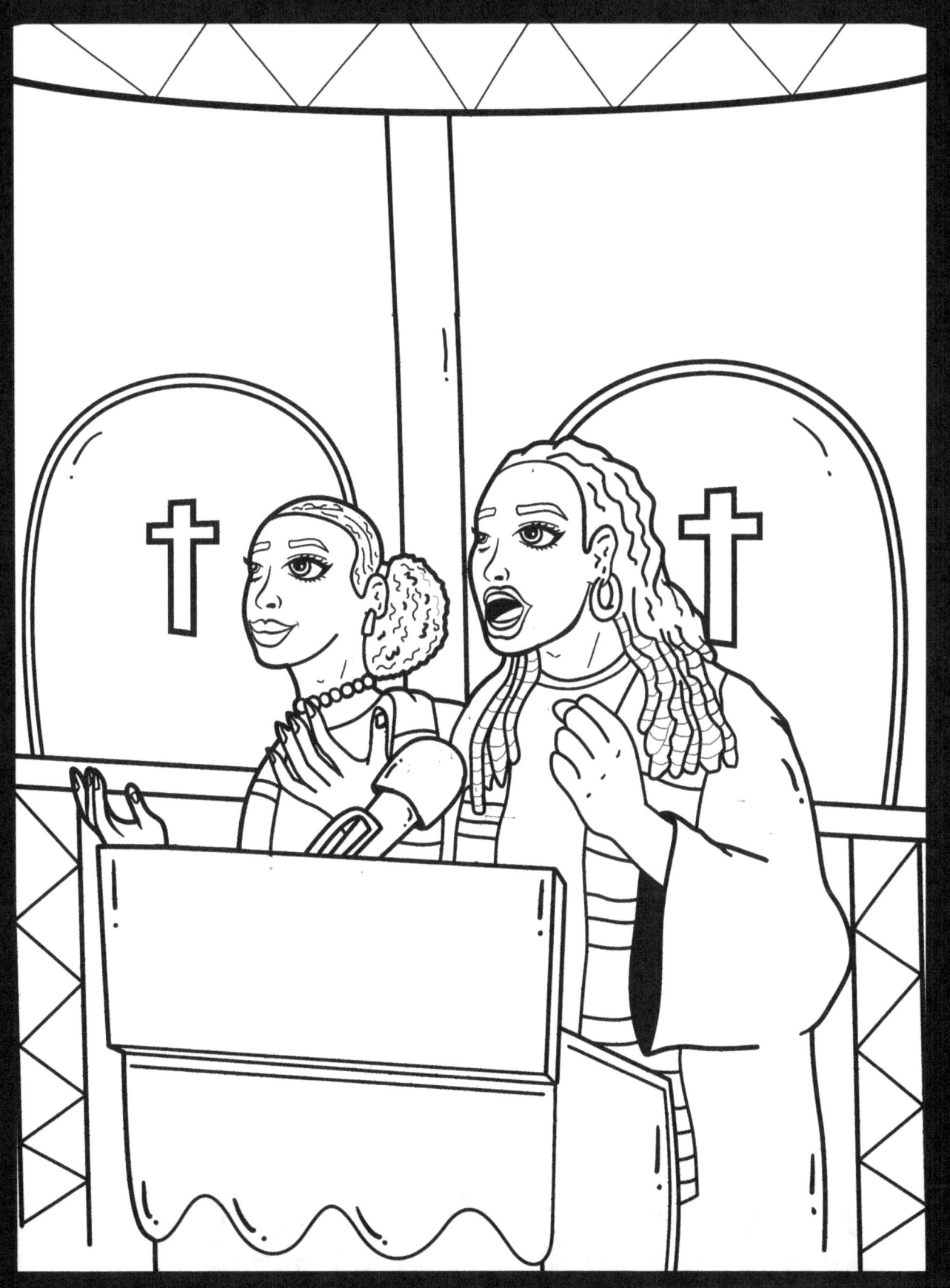

# GOSPEL SINGERS

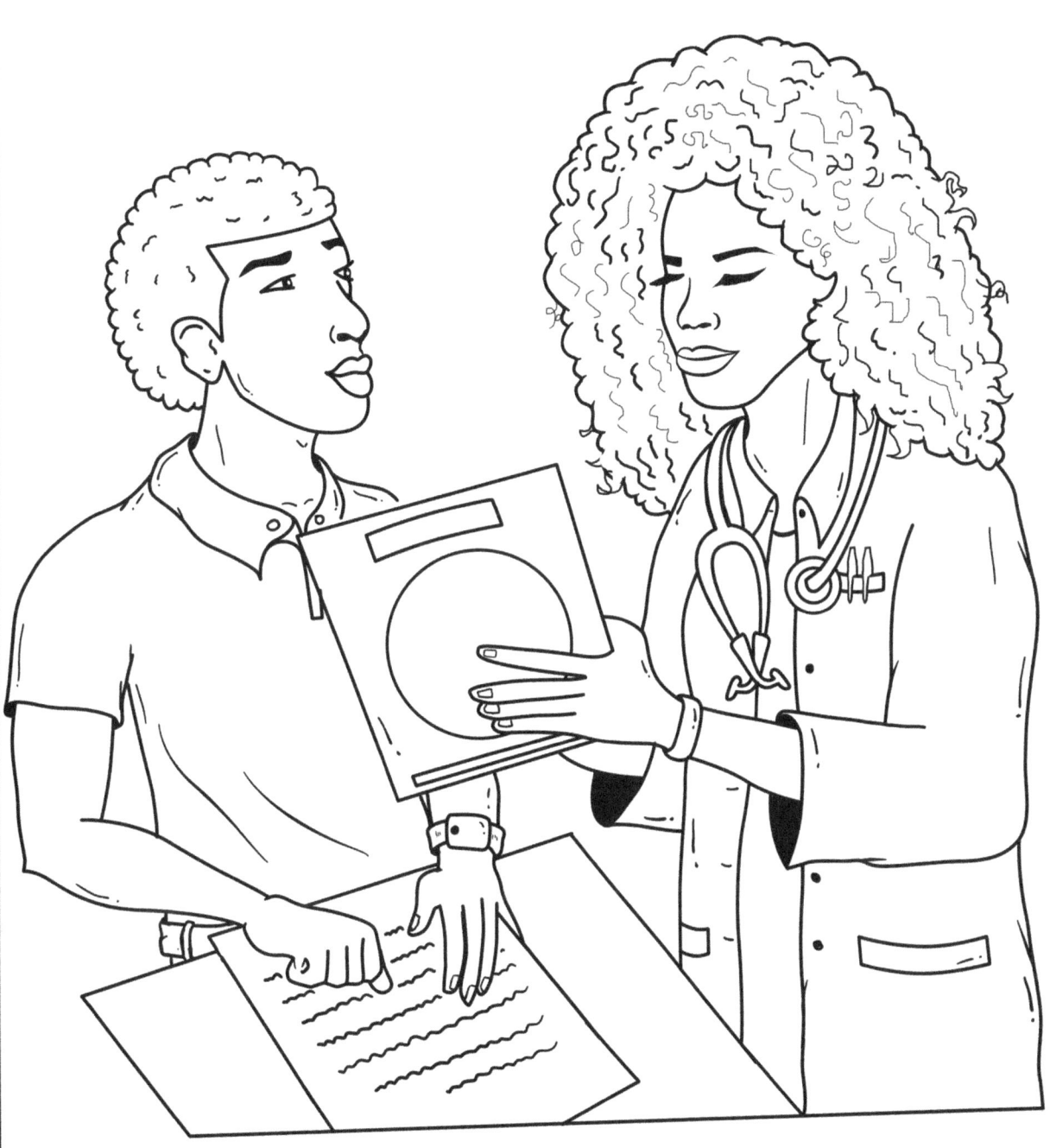

# DOCTOR'S APPOINTMENT

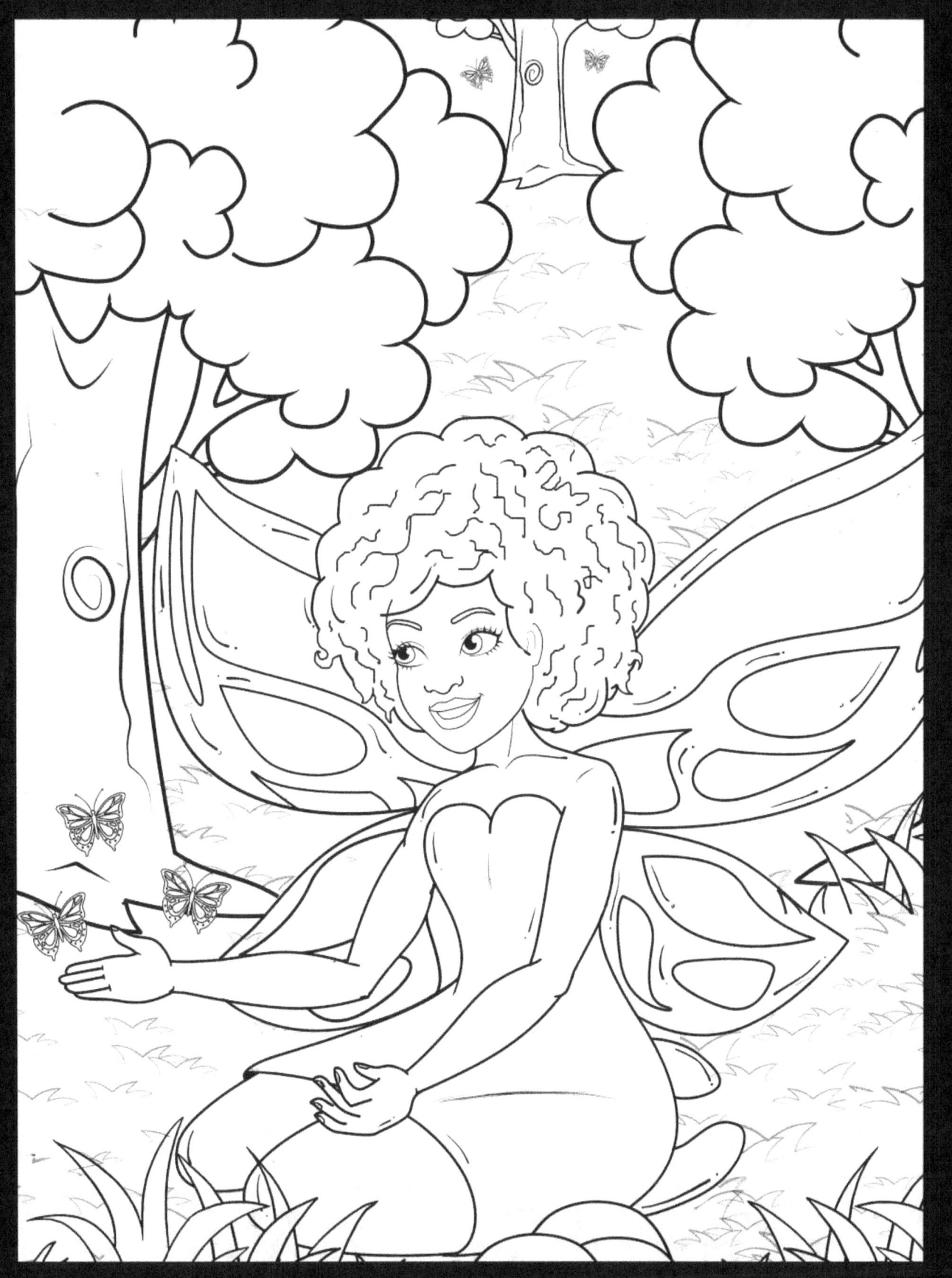

# FANTASY LAND

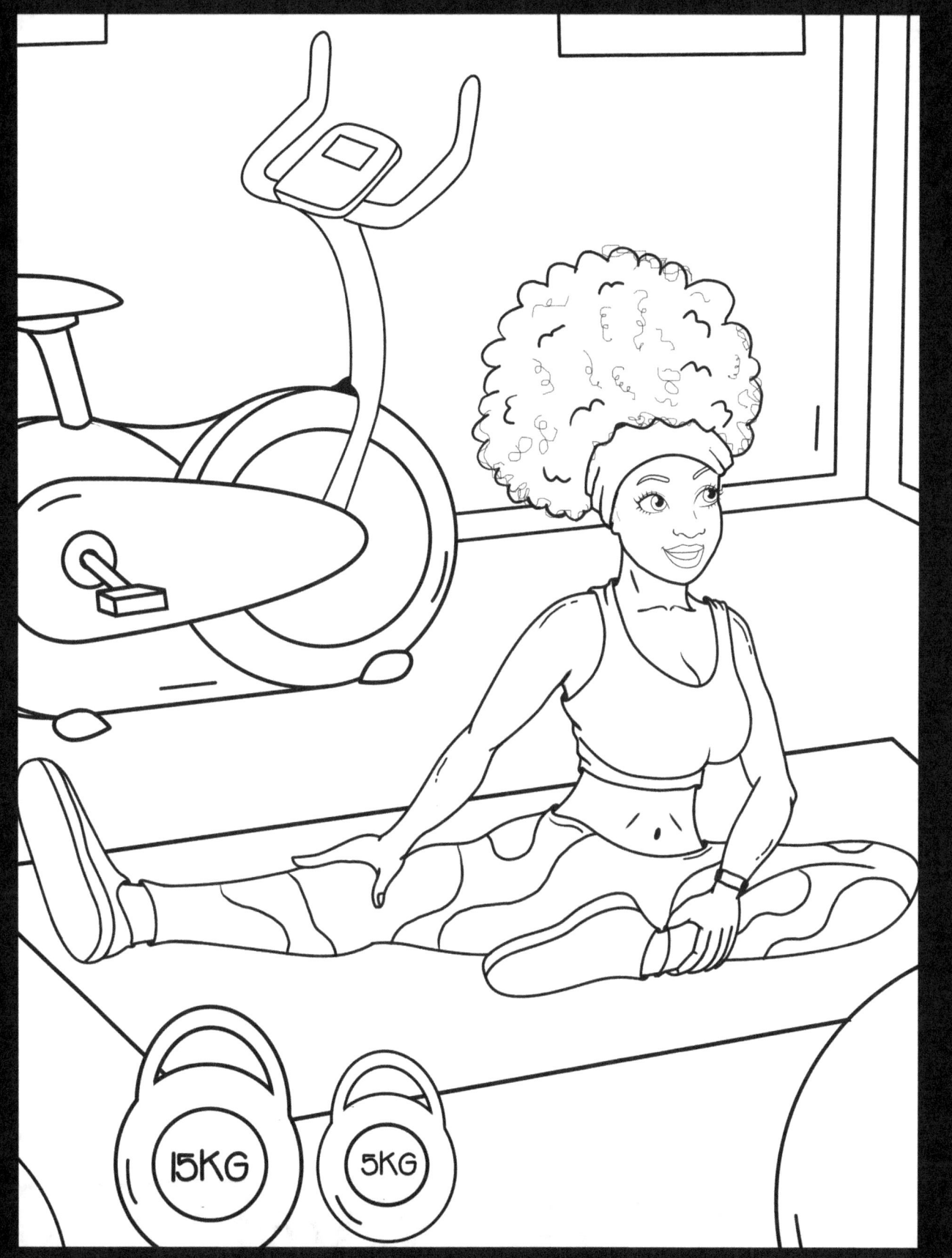

# AT THE GYM

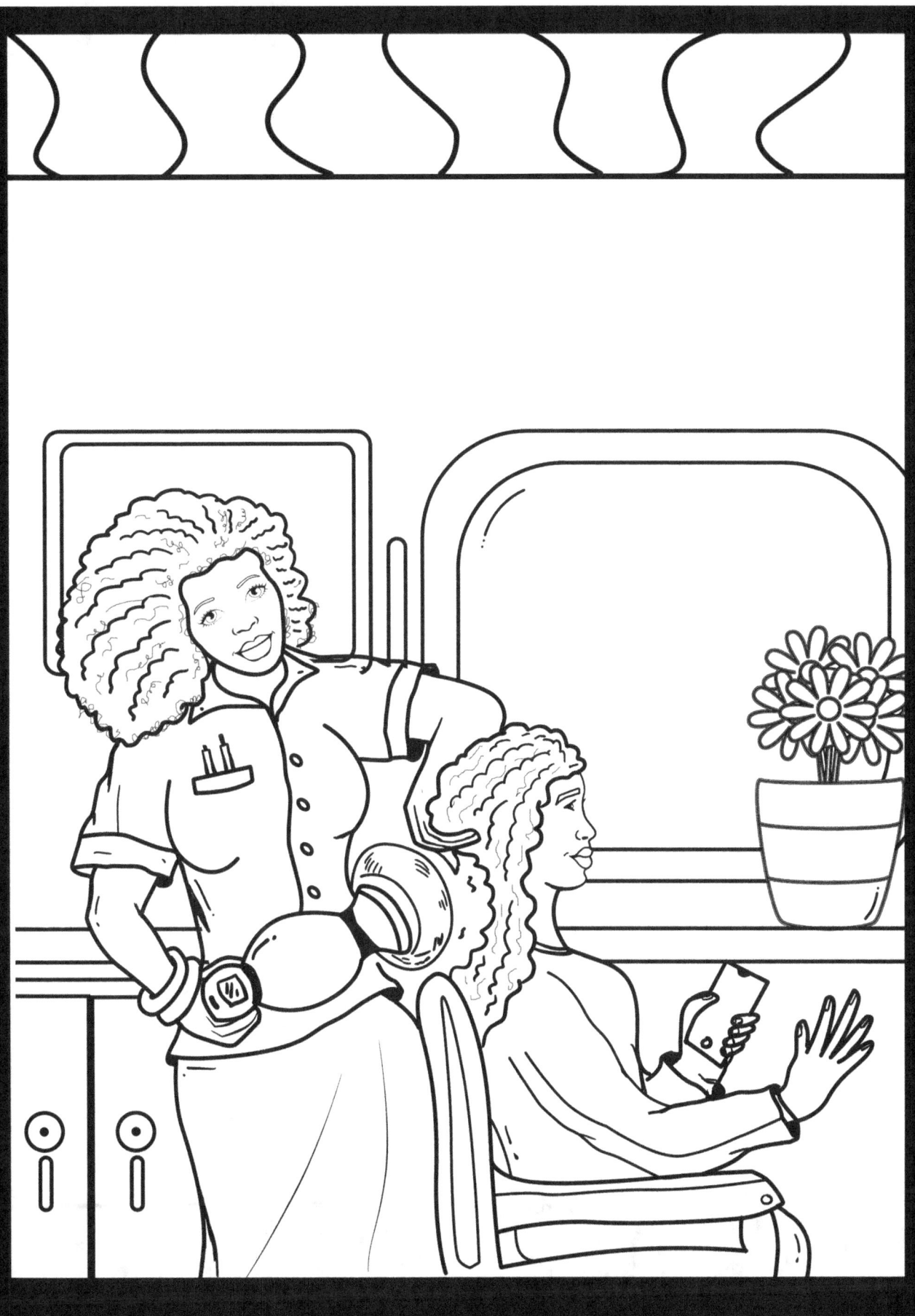

# HAIR APPOINTMENT

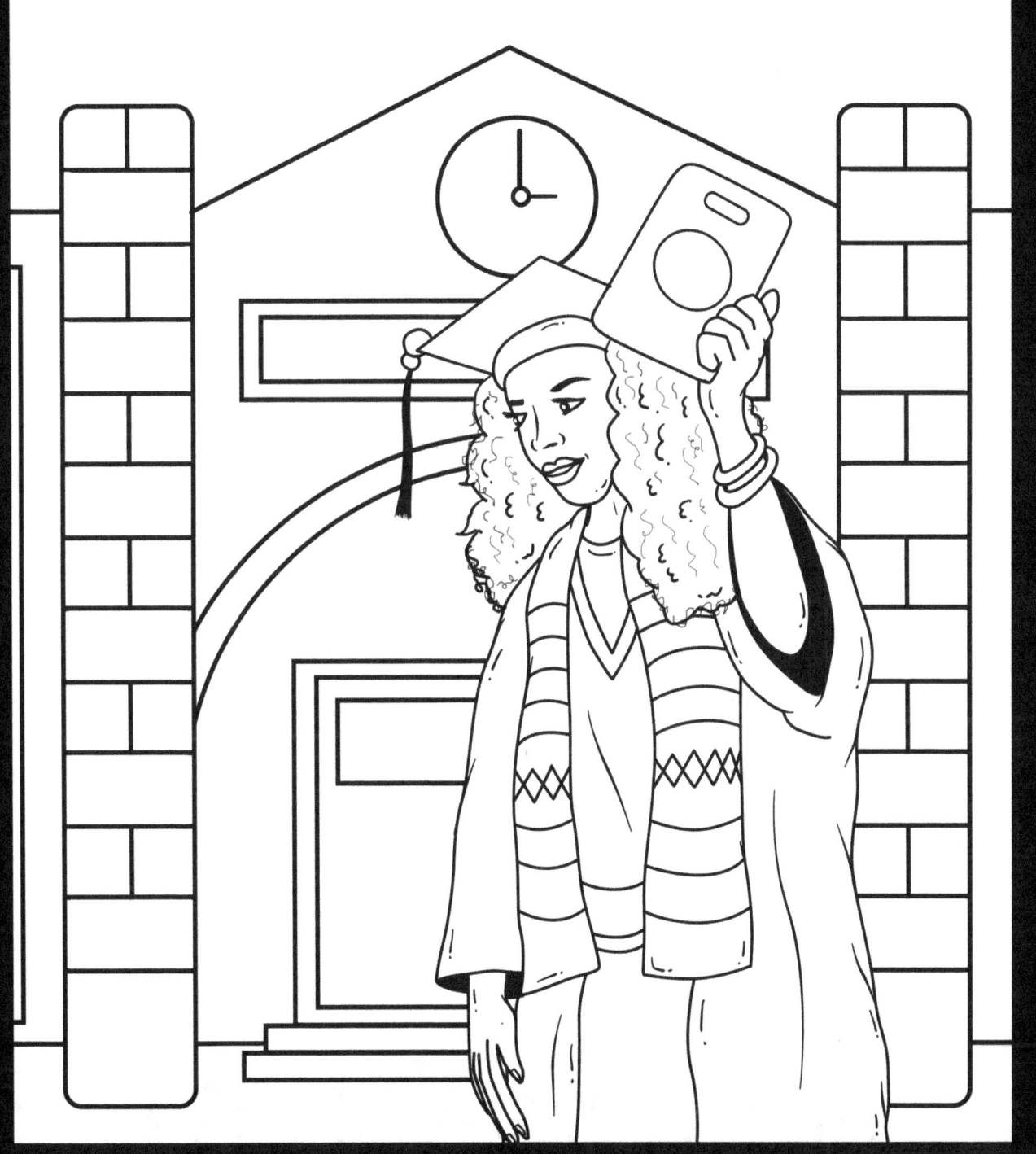

# HBCU GRADUATE

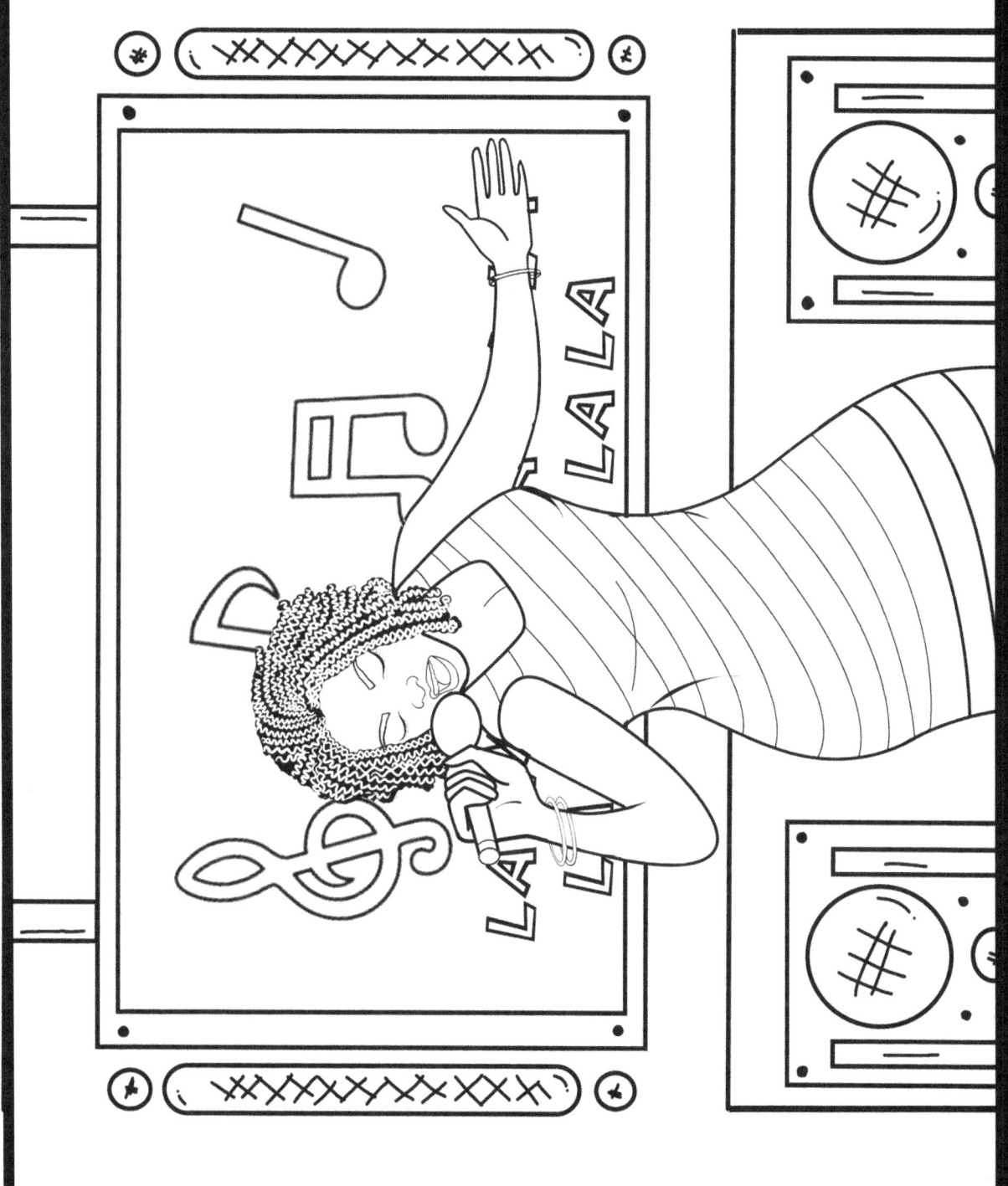

# GOT SOUL?

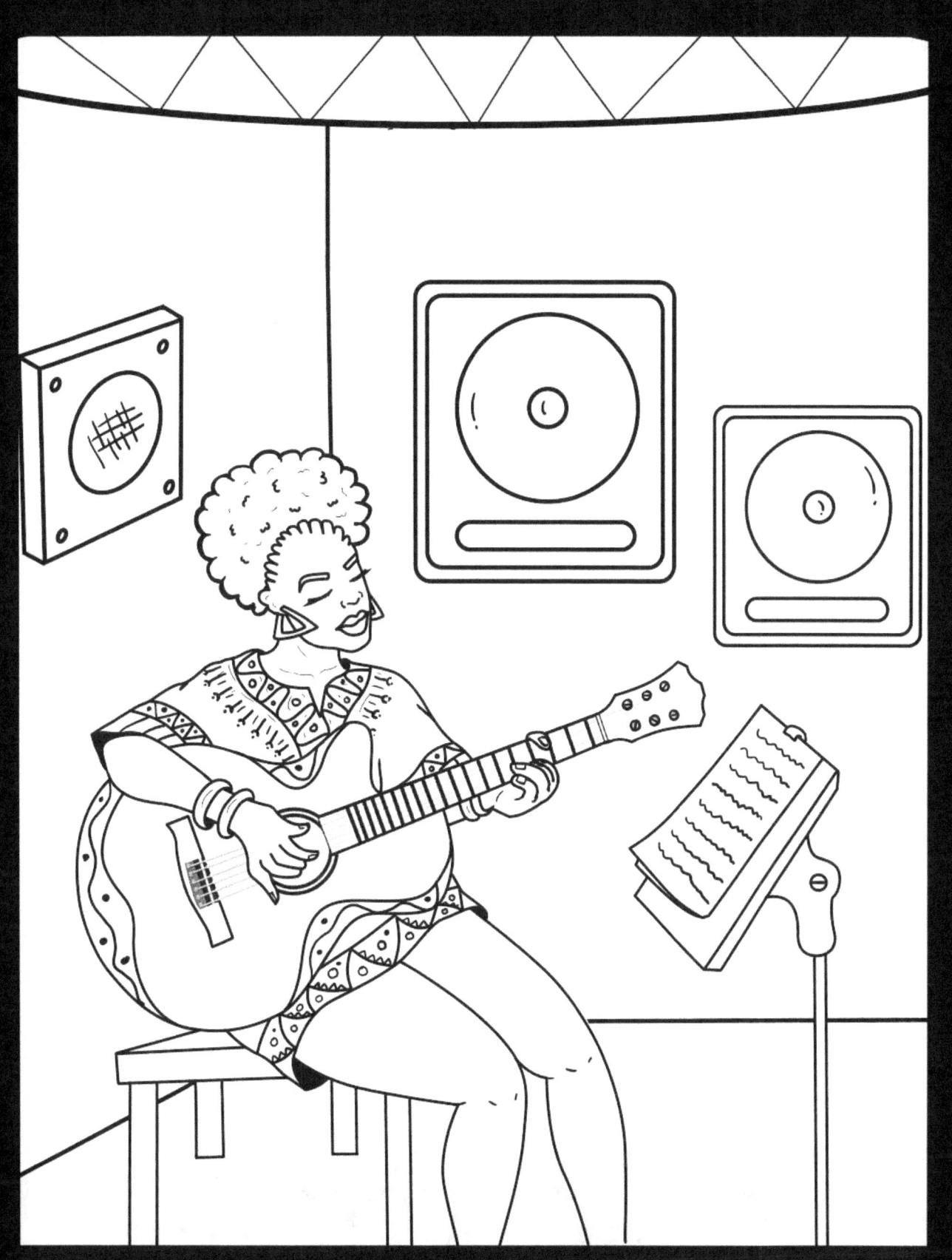

# SONG WRITER

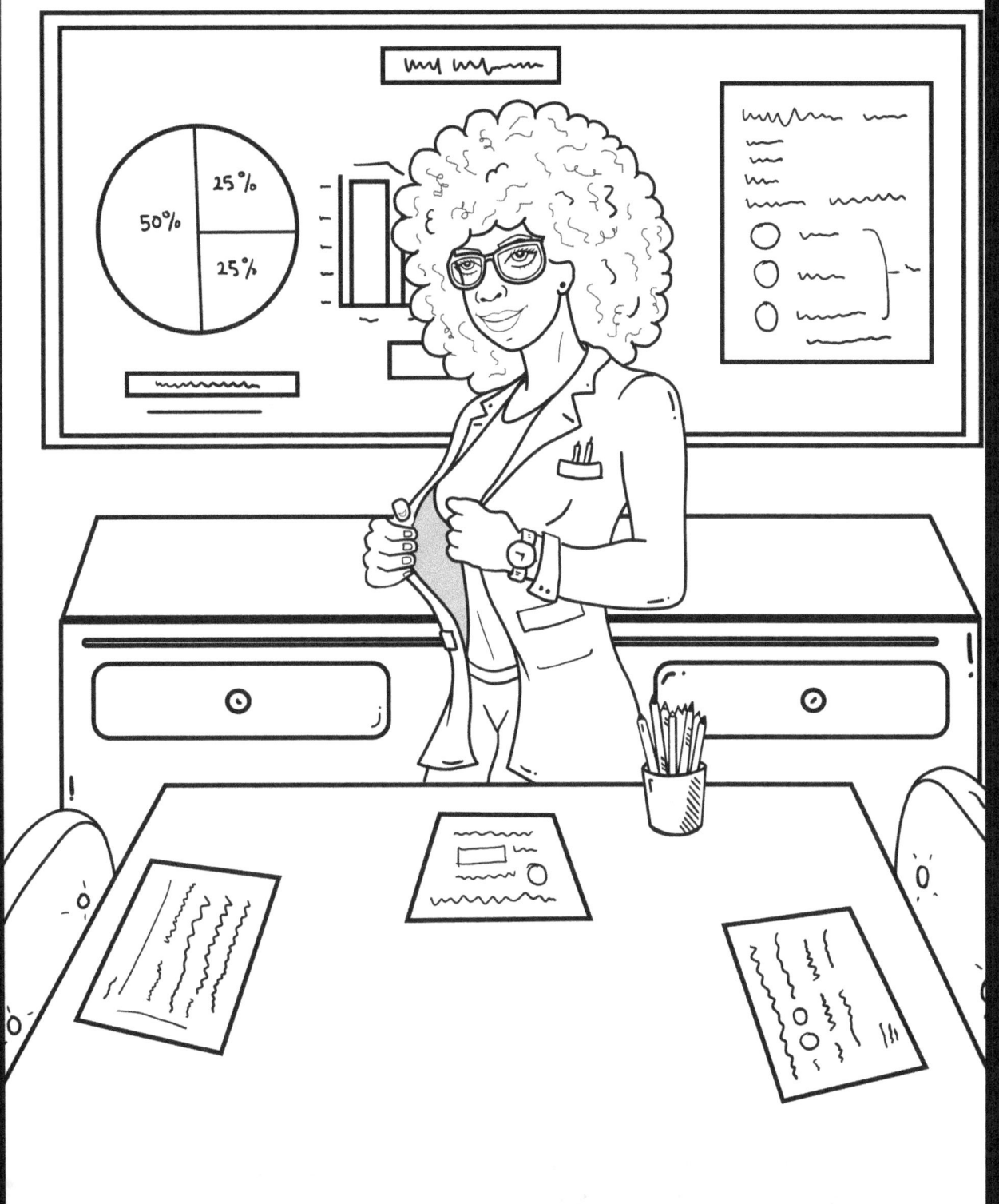

BLACK BUSINESS WOMAN

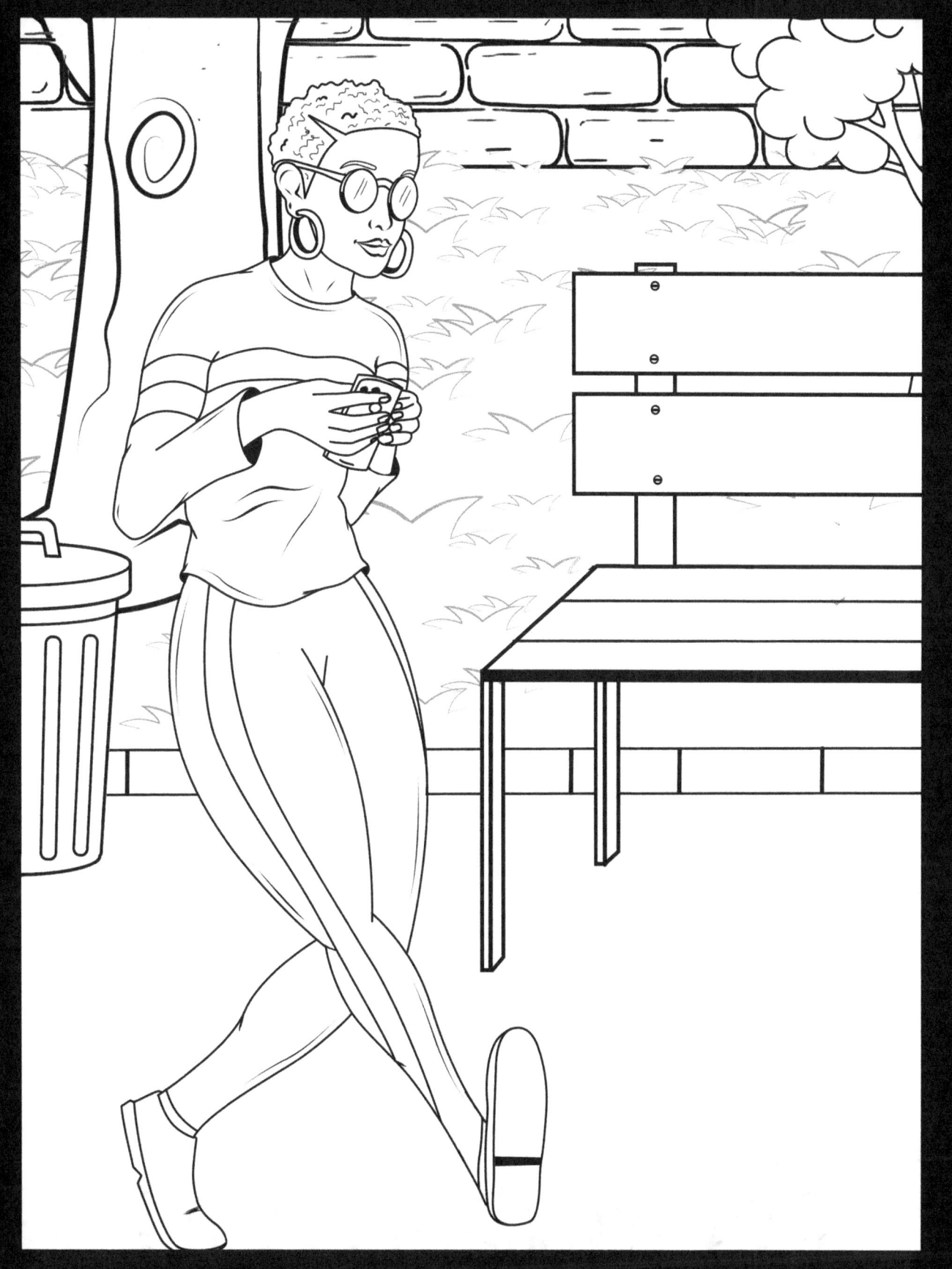

# EVENING STROLL

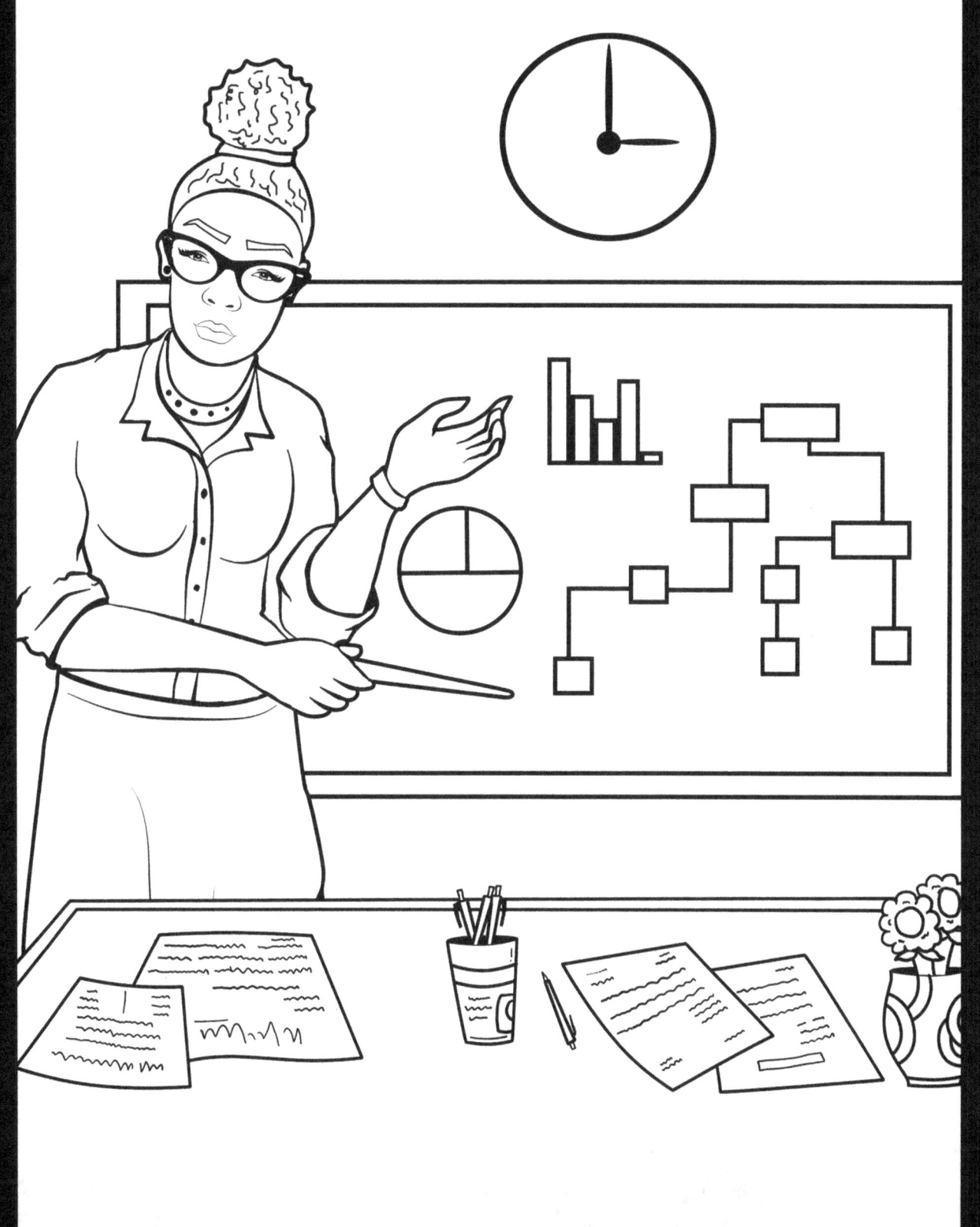

# PRESENTATION

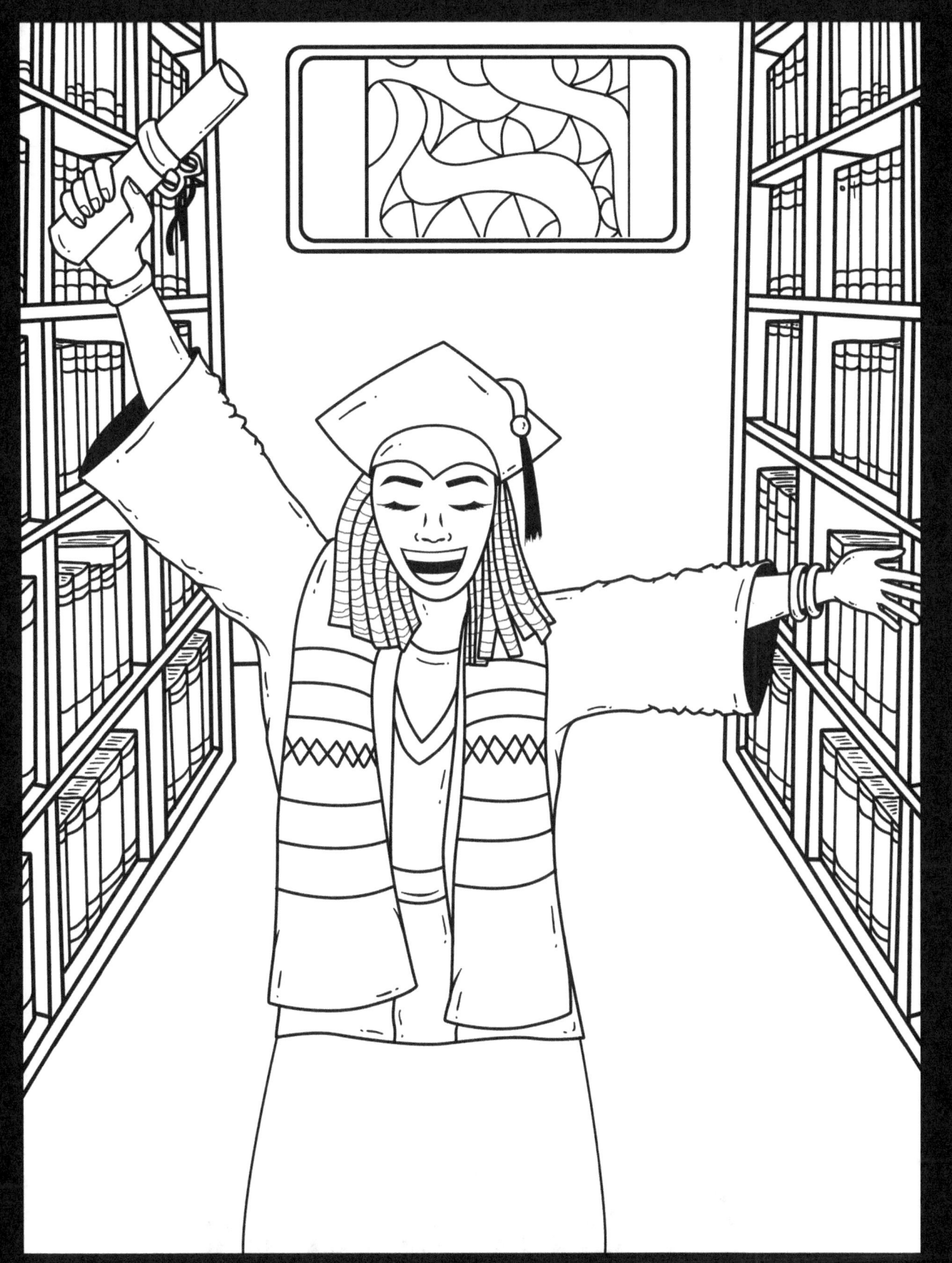

# GRADUATION

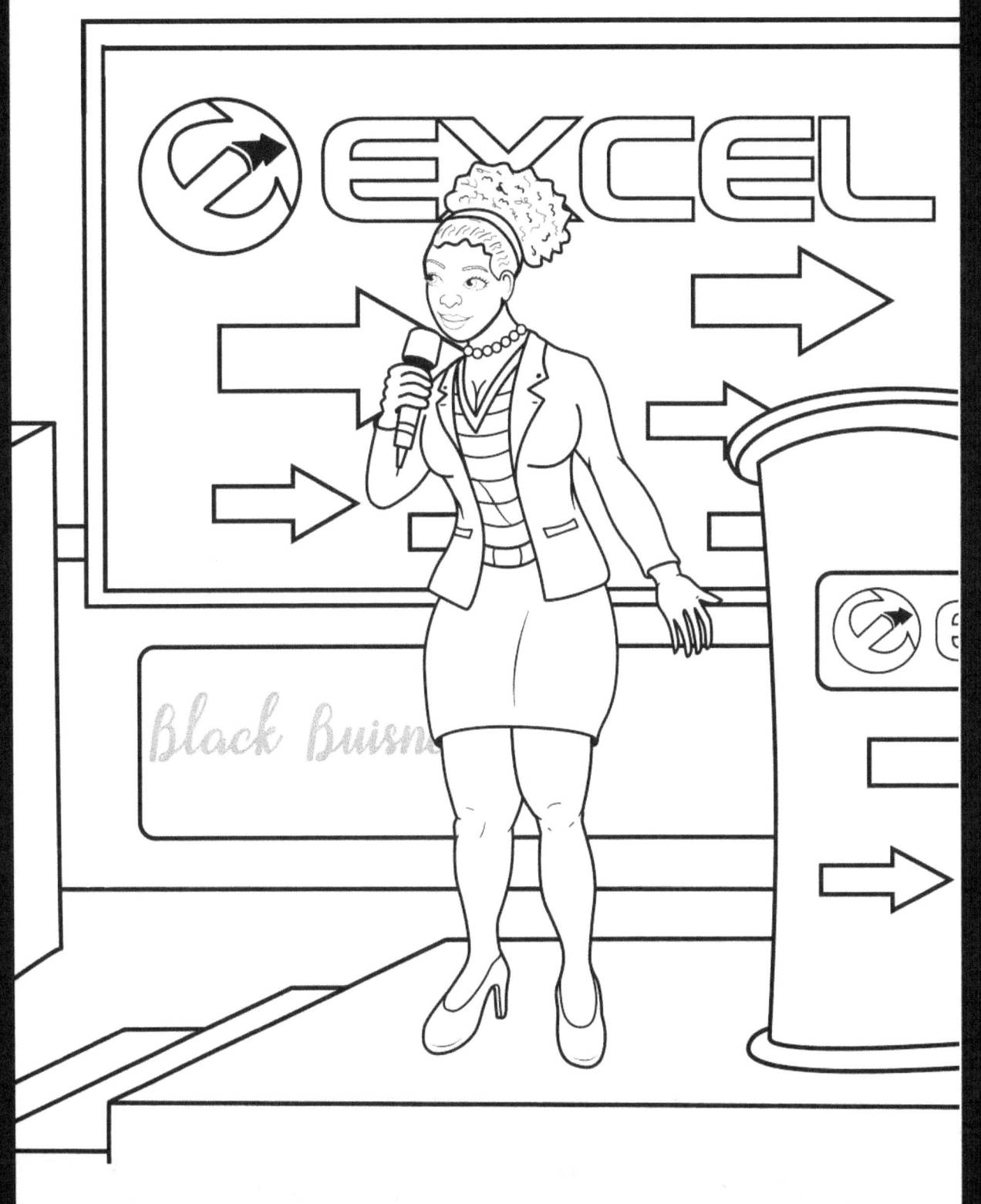

PUBLIC SPEAKER

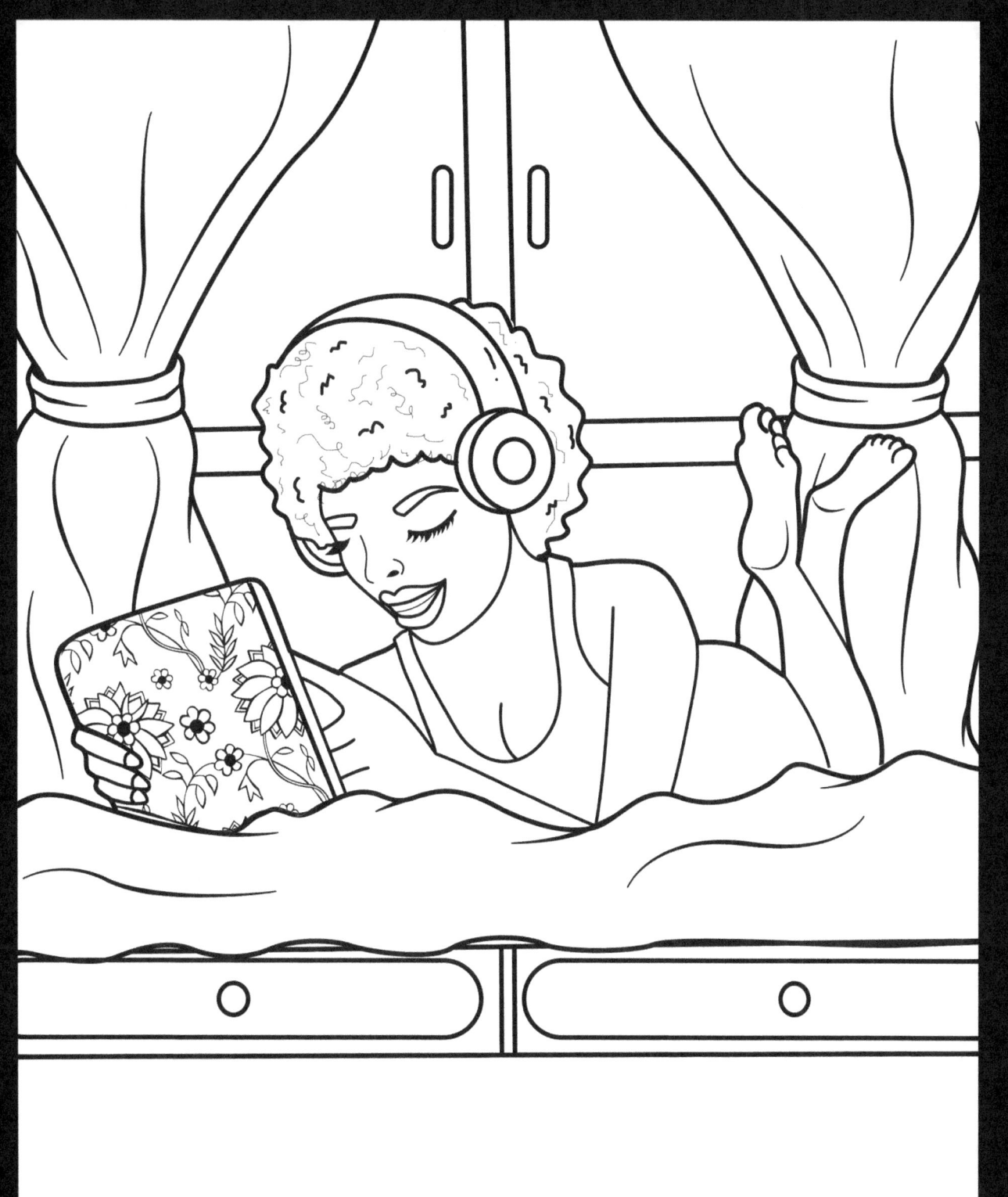

# CHILLING IN MY ROOM

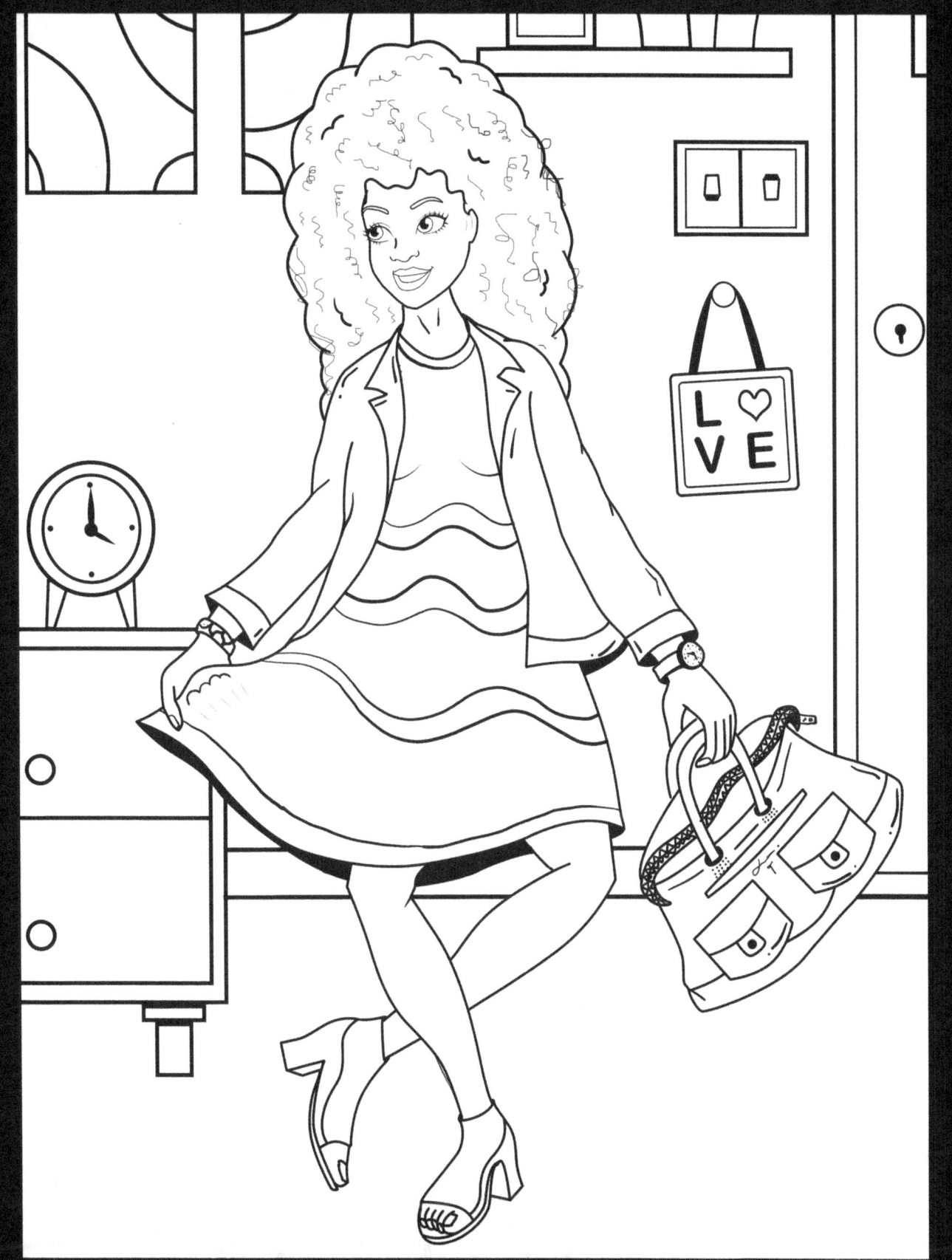

# GOING OUT

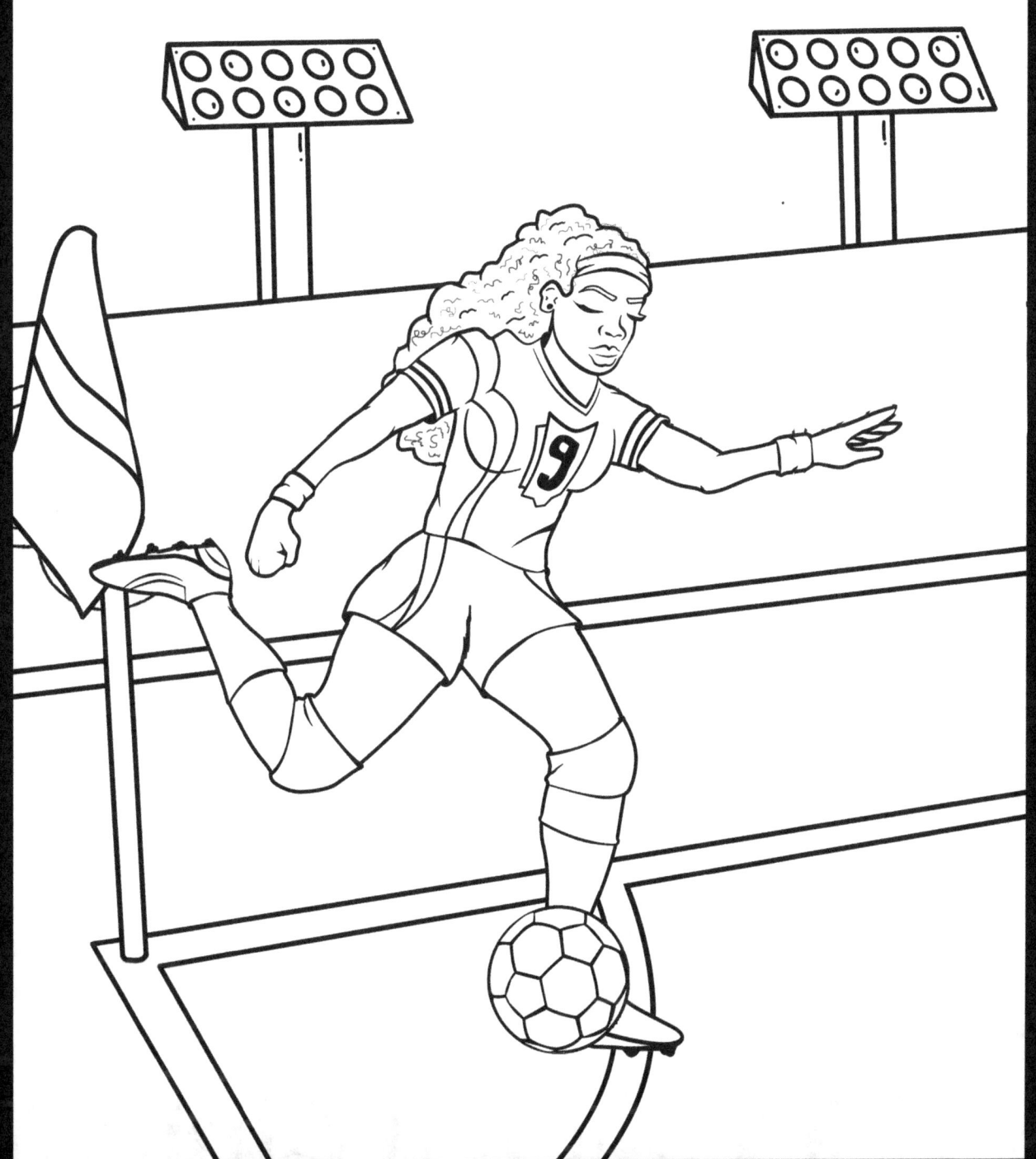

KICK LIKE A GIRL

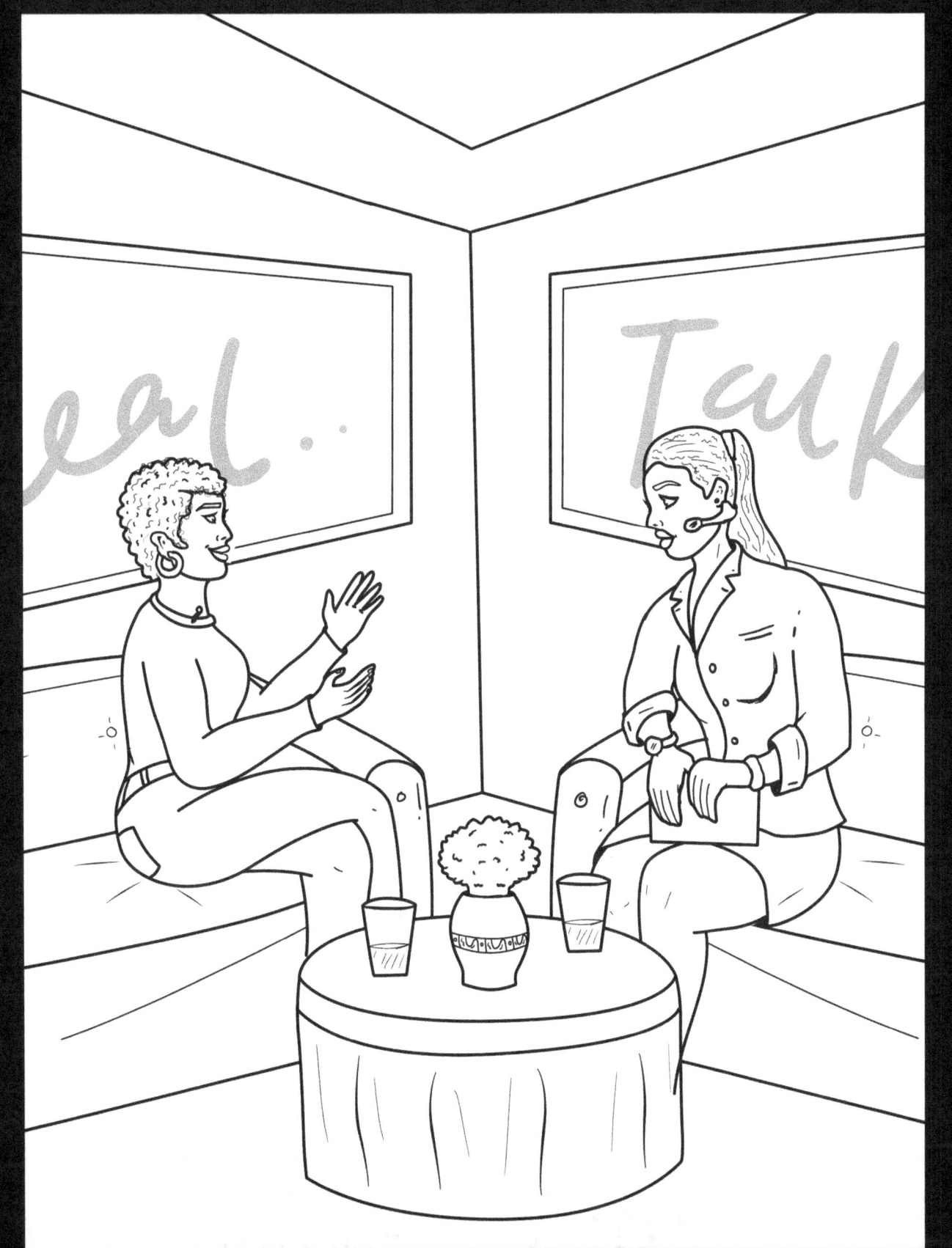

# TALK SHOW

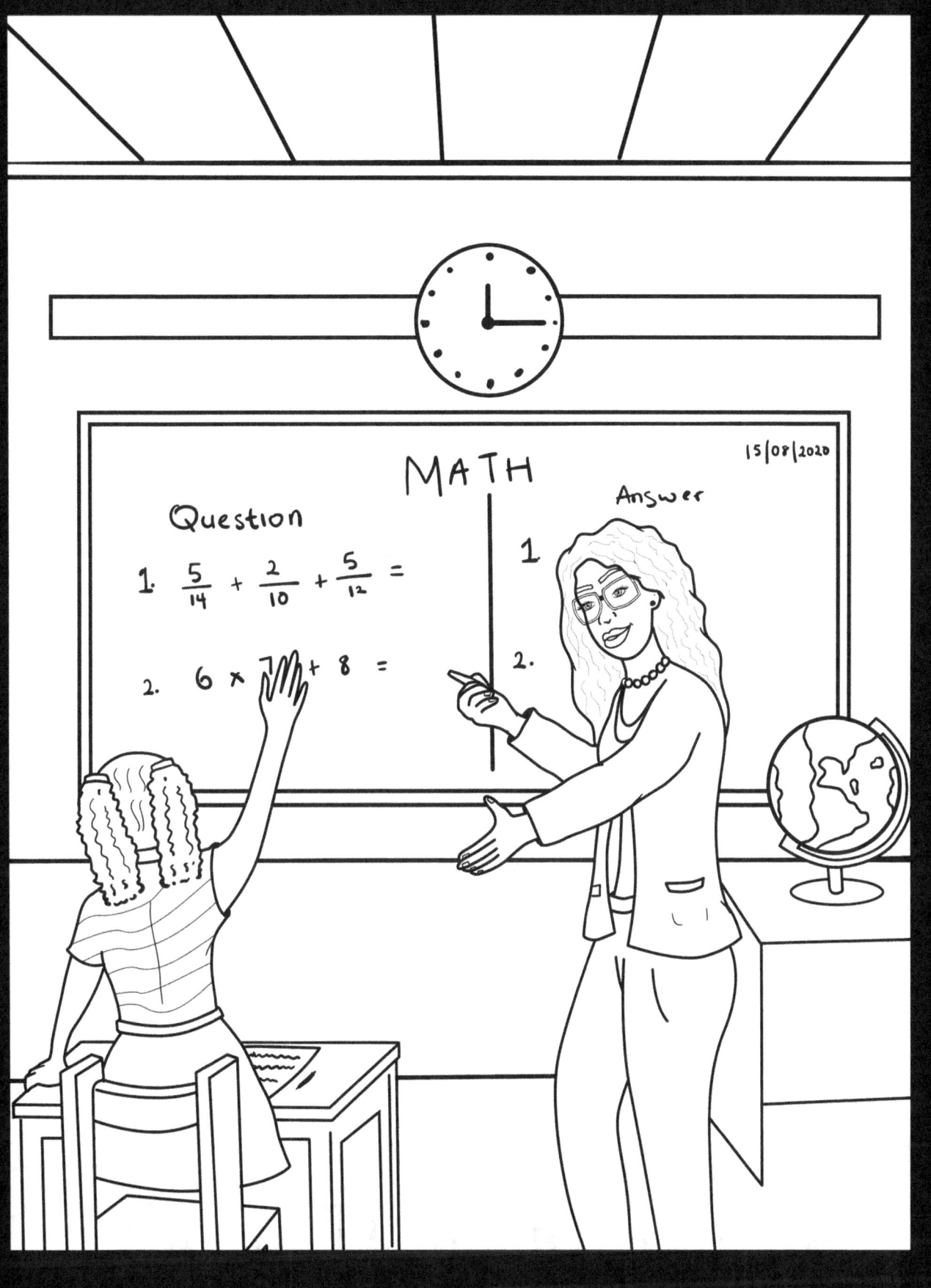

# HIGH SCHOOL TEACHER

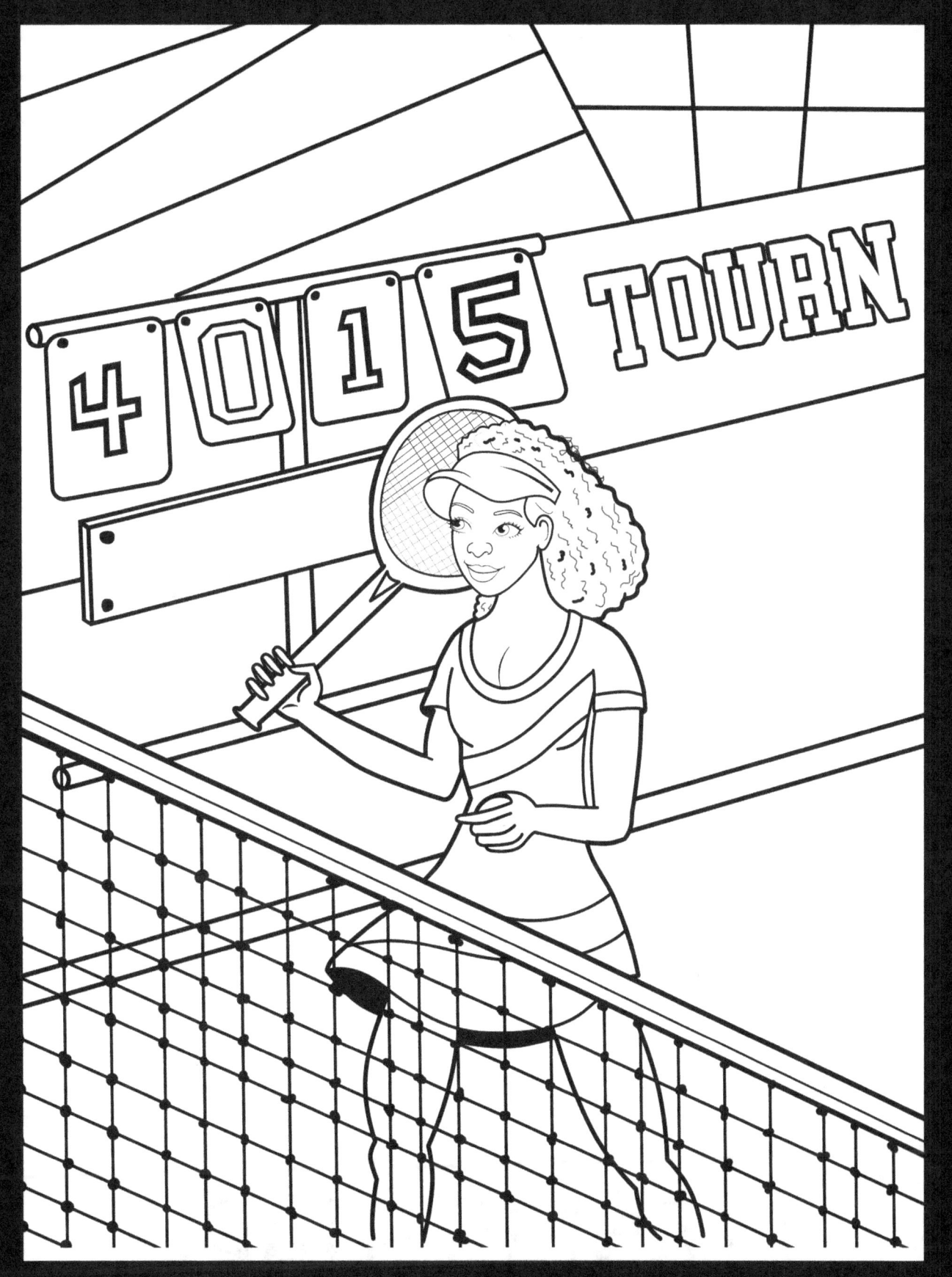

# TENNIS STAR

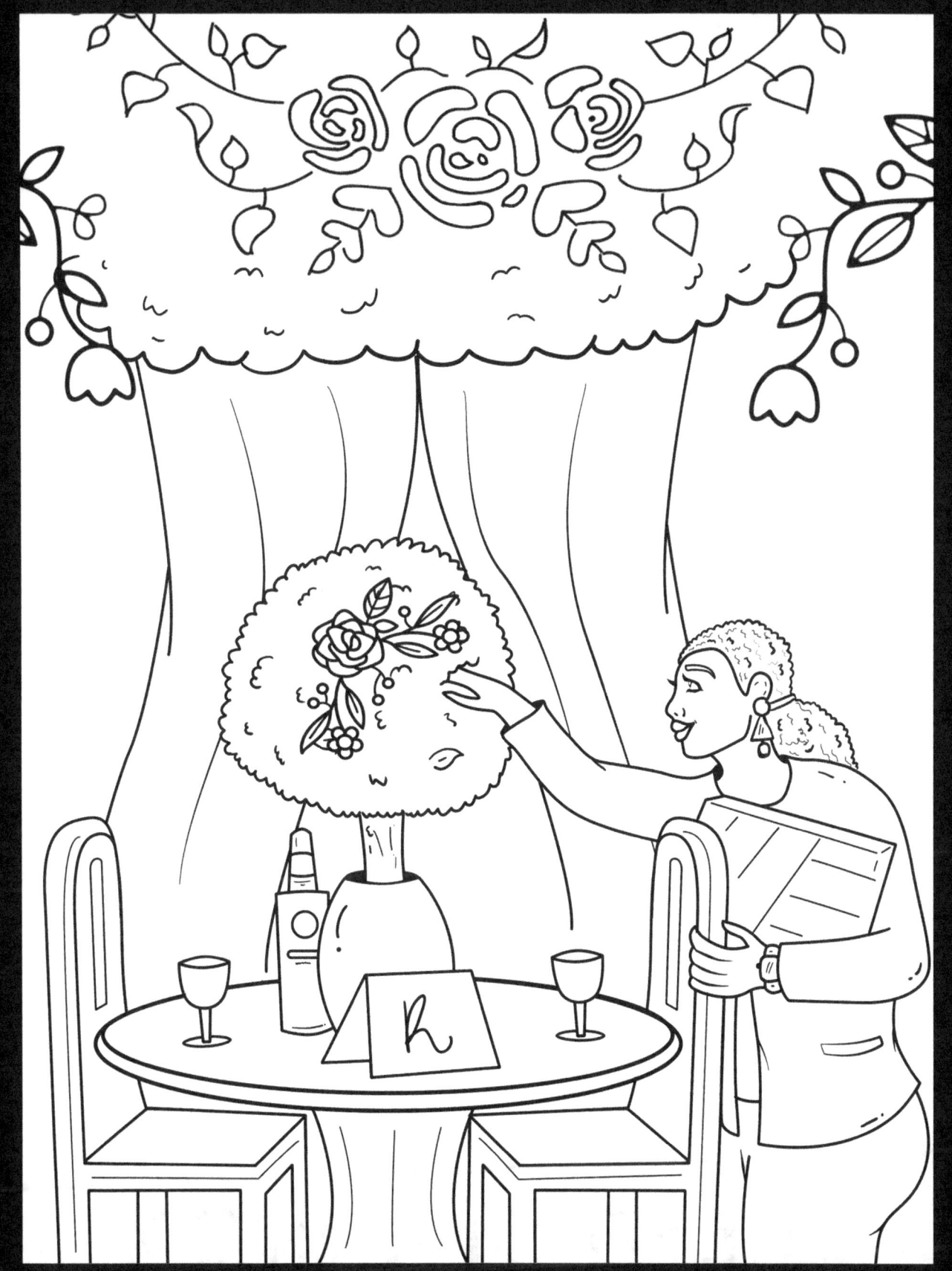

# EVENT PLANNER

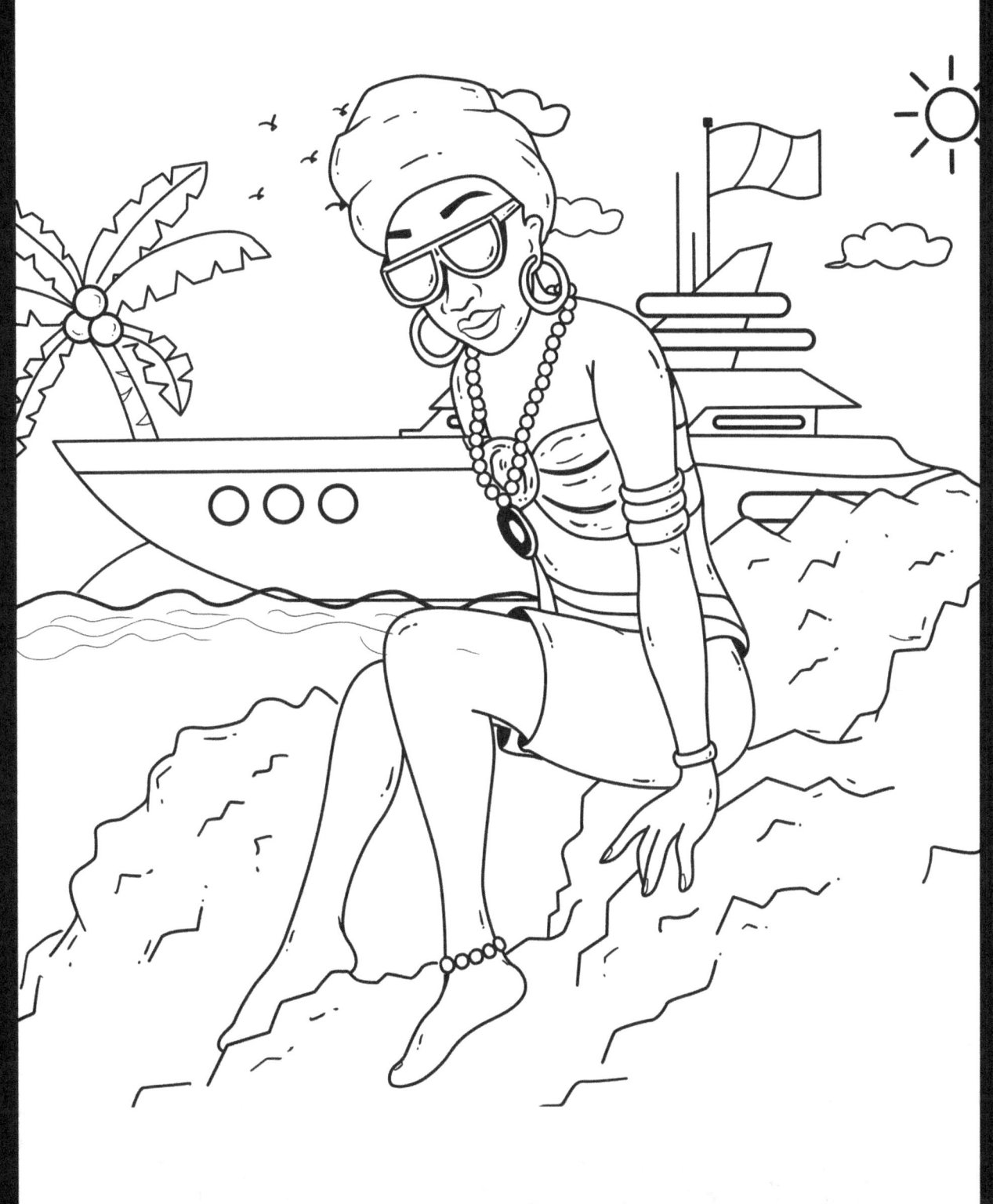

# CARIBBEAN CRUISE

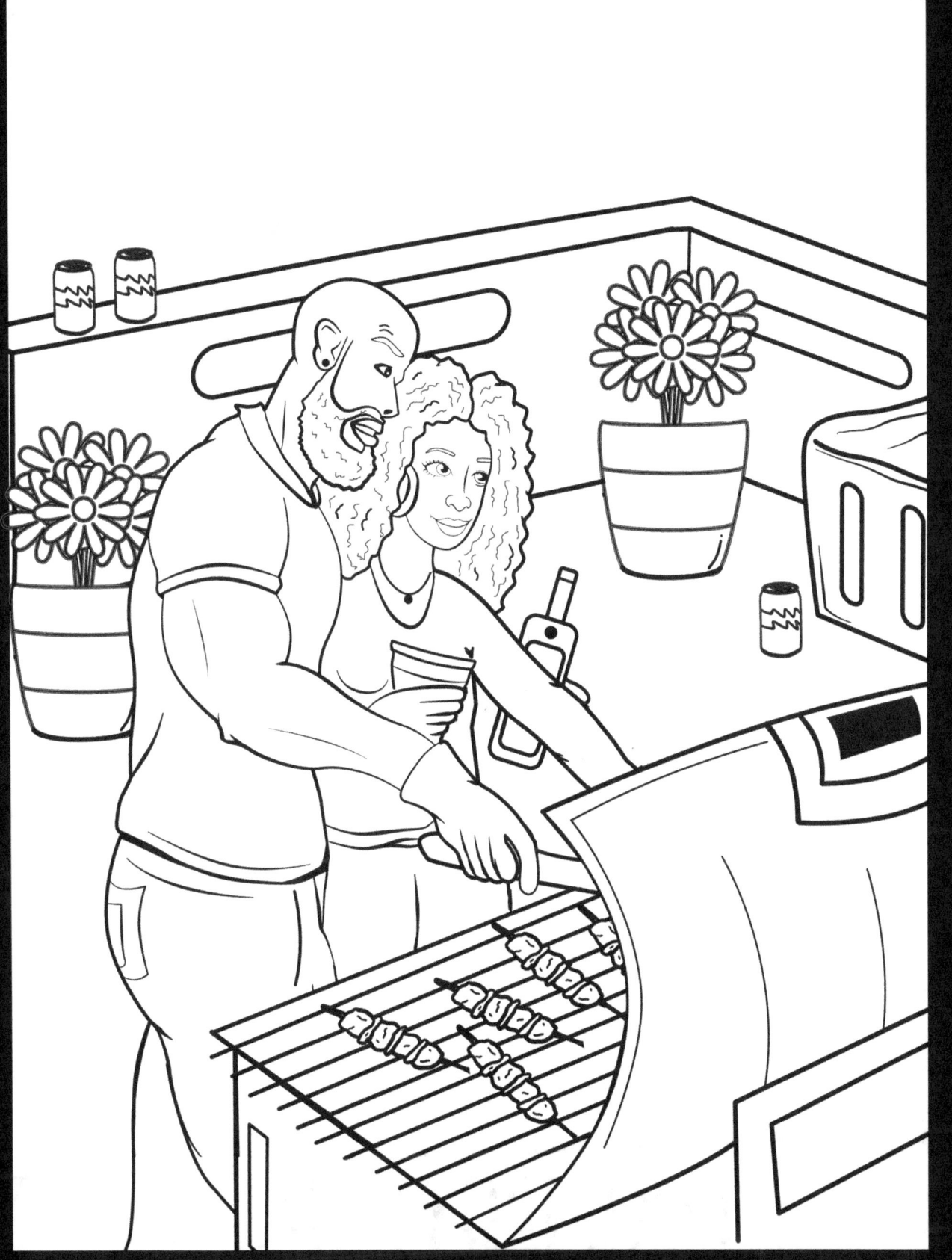

# BARBECUE

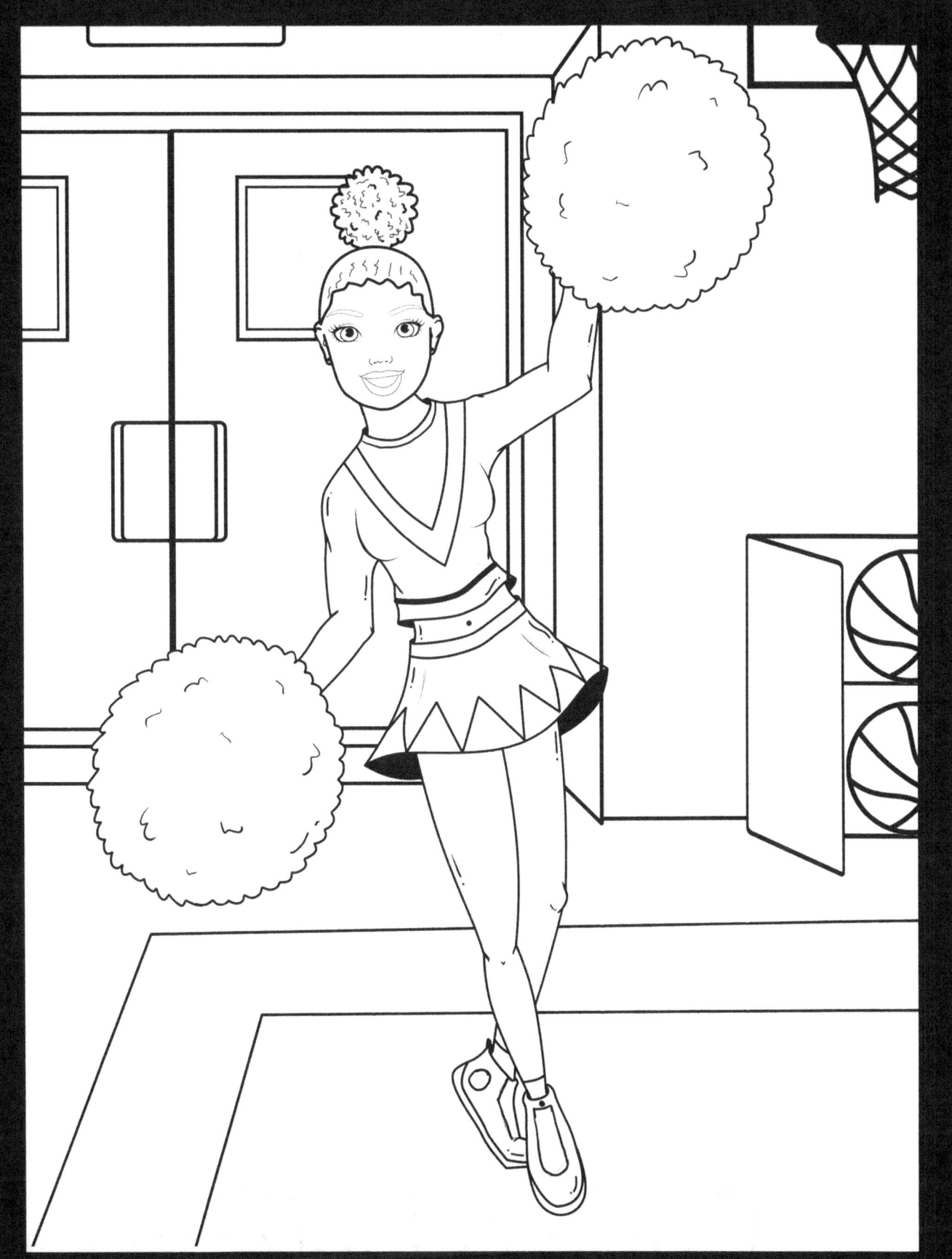

# CHEERLEADER

# ABOUT THE ARTIST

Sandra Mcdyess is an artist, illustrator and writer. She licenses her illustrations on all kinds of products including books, tshirts, mugs and stickers.

Black Women Are Dope is the first coloring book created by Sandra Mcdyess, but there will be many to come :)

www.delitefulcoloring.com